SUMI JO

조수미

Daniel Choy | Yun Hyeji

 영진미디어

SUMI JO

Daniel Choy | Yun Hyeji

OZEKO 영진미디어

이 책의 난이도

이 책은 '영어로 읽는 세계 속 한국인' 시리즈입니다. 초등학교 고학년에서 중학생까지 읽기에 적당한 수준이며, 뒤쪽으로 갈수록 어휘가 다양해집니다. 12세~15세 청소년 **대상**의 TOEFL Junior를 준비하고 있는 학생들이 보기에 적절합니다.

초등학교 고학년			중학생		
11세	12세	13세	14세	15세	16세

기준	난이도
단어	2000 단어 내외
문법	시제를 구분하고 구와 절의 문장 구조를 이해할 수 있는 정도
독해	글을 읽고 정확한 내용을 파악하여, 질문에 답하거나 다음 내용을 추론할 수 있는 종합적인 사고력을 지닌 정도

※ 청담 어학원의 Tera, Bridge, Par 레벨, 토피아 어학원의 HT4, GB, G1 레벨, 아발론 어학원의 JB, JI, JA 레벨 정도의 학생들이 보기에 적절합니다.

PREFACE

'The series of Korean in the world to read in English',
is a series of stories about famous Koreans from various
walks of life presenting their lives and achievements in
English. This book is an easy and fun read for young
people, its major class of readers, and a great way both
to learn English and to find out more about today's
heroes and what makes them so great.

Each chapter consists of beautifully illustrated pages.
As the book is composed only in English, the reader
is able to read and understand the English language at

his or her own pace, mastering vocabulary, sentence structure and reading skills. The accompanied CD recording of the text will improve listening while the downloadable PDF version of the Korean text will help with comprehension. The text is available at the YoungJinMedia website at www.yjbooks.co.kr and the FILE recording of the text is available at the YongjinMedia IBlug at yjmedia.iblug.com.

The sixth story of this series is about Jo Sumi. This prima donna swept 6 international competitions and became the first Asian to perform as the lead in the world's most prestigious opera houses. She is still pursuing her musical endeavors, and continues to delight her fans and supporters. This is the real life story of the singer who is praised as the voice of heaven.

CONTENTS

Korea's finest prima donna Jo Sumi,
her pursuit of musical excellence continues.

1. God Given Voice

It is no **exaggeration**▪ to say everyone in Korea must have heard of Jo Sumi's <Der Holle Rache Kocht in meinem Herzen(Queen of the Night's Aria)> at least once. It's the song that first springs to mind when Koreans think of opera. Jo Sumi, who sang that song is one of the most recognized and respected singers in the world of opera.

Prima donna means the first lady in Italian.

▪ **exaggeration** [igzædʒəréiʃən] ⓝ overstatement

The **term** describes the most valued soprano singer in an opera. Today, in any performances, Jo Sumi is easily recognized by that title. There are very few sopranos in the world that can perform <Queen of the Night's Aria> to perfection. And among them, Jo Sumi is easily considered the best.

Maestro Herbert von Karajan who loved and respected Sumi dearly, eagerly praised her as the singer with the voice of heaven. He could never compliment Sumi enough, as he knew that other than talent, she works harder than anyone.

Asian singers are born with **disadvantages** in many ways. Asians have smaller **physique** and lung capacity compared to Europeans. These

---

- **term** [tə:rm] ⓝ,ⓥ a word or expression used for some particular thing
- **disadvantage** [dìsədvǽntidʒ] ⓝ,ⓥ the quality of having an inferior or less favorable position
- **physique** [fizí:k] ⓝ constitution of the human body

factors and more, make it harder for Asians to become successful opera singers. Naturally, Sumi faced numerous obstacles and had to endure difficult and painful times to reach the top in the opera world. She hung in there, believing that **dedication**▪ and **perseverance**▪ prevails all. Hard work and **determination**▪ helped her become the prima donna she is today.

▪ **dedication** [dèdikéiʃən] ⓝ complete and wholehearted fidelity

▪ **perseverance** [pəˈrsəvíərəns] ⓝ persistent determination

▪ **determination** [ditəˈrmənéiʃən] ⓝ the act of making up your mind about something

2. Fueled by Compliments

"Aww! Sookyong, is there anything you can't do?"

"Look at this painting! You should become an artist!"

"How can you play the piano so well with those tiny hands?""

"You have such an **angelic**▪ voice! You'll make a fine singer one day!"

Sumi's real name is Jo Sookyong. She changed

▪ **angelic** [ændʒélik] ⓐ marked by utter benignity; resembling or befitting an angel or saint

her name to Sumi during her international debut because most foreigners had difficulty pronouncing her real name. Some advised her to **switch**▪ to an English name instead, but Sumi **refused**▪ to do so, as she was proud to be a Korean.

The biggest contributing factor in Sumi's success is her parent's unending praise. They only had kind and encouraging words for their daughter. Children are full of dreams. At one moment, they might dream of becoming an artist, a singer the next and a teacher or a president afterwards. And Sumi was no different. But her parents supported her dreams no matter how often she'd change her mind. Their love and support helped Sumi grow up

---

▪ **switch** [swiʧ] ⓝ,ⓥ change over, change around, as to a new order or sequence

▪ **refuse** [rifjúːz] ⓝ,ⓥ show unwillingness towards

to be the brave and confident person she is today. Sumi's mother always respected the little girl's opinions. Sumi started talking at a rather early age, and she was very **talkative**▪ and full of questions. But no matter how much the little girl **bugged**▪ her, Sumi's mother was patient and understanding always. Not even once, did she lose her temper. She always spoke gently and kindly to her curious and talkative little girl. Sumi learned from her kind and gentle mother, how to be patient and polite with others.

Sumi's mother was quite a music lover. She was a big fan of Maria Callas who was known as 'the diva of the opera' at that time. Believing that

---

▪ **talkative** [tɔ́ːkətiv] ⓐ full of trivial conversation

▪ **bug** [bʌg] ⓝ,ⓥ annoy persistently

music is good for the mental well-being of her baby, she always listened to music while she was pregnant with Sumi. So it's no surprise that Sumi sang before she could even speak. Sumi's mother played a big role in **fostering**▪ her musical talent.

Sumi started talking and reading at a very early age. Even when she was a baby, she could articulately read newspaper articles, much to the delight and surprise of her mother.

"Sookyong! You can read!"

"Yes I can."

"You are so clever. You learned reading by yourself!"

"I sing better than I read."

▪ **foster** [fɔ́ːstər] ⓐ,ⓝ,ⓥ promote the growth of

"Is that so? Then let's hear it."

Sumi's mother loved various types of music, regardless of its genre, classical or popular. The sound of music from the radio **echoed**▪ through her home, always. And Sumi would listen and sing along. Sumi was able to perform those songs perfectly before her mother.

"Sookyong! Where did you learn to sing these songs? You have such a beautiful voice! I'm so surprised!"

Sumi's mother was deeply impressed. This little girl could sing with a perfect pitch. But more importantly, her songs were charged with true emotions. That's something no girl of that age can do.

▪ **echo** [ékou] ⓝ,ⓥ ring or echo with sound

Sumi's mother, who loved literature and the arts once dreamed of becoming a singer when she was young. But to focus on being a homemaker and provide for her family, she had to give up that dream.

'My Sookyong has what it takes to be a great singer. I'll do all I can to help her become a world-class singer.'

She wanted to give Sumi a headstart in developing her musical talent. She taught Sumi to play the piano to help her understand music better. A piano is very expensive and few homes could afford it. Sumi's family could not afford such expensive items. But Sumi's mother did all she can to make sure they could have a piano for Sumi. Sumi's mother even leaned to play the piano herself to encourage her daughter. Sumi was able to recognize and remember any notes she played. It became clear that she was born to be a musician. She was also blessed with the **ability** to **mimic** any song instantly. These talents deeply impressed Sumi's piano teacher. She **urged** Sumi's mother to make sure Sumi can study music further.

■ **ability** [əbíləti] ⓝ the quality of being able to perform

■ **mimic** [mímik] ⓝ,ⓥ,ⓐ imitate, especially for satirical effect

■ **urge** [ə:rdʒ] ⓝ,ⓥ push for something

3. Untamed Sumi

Fans of Jo Sumi instantly link her to a beautiful diva. A feminine figure in a long, beautiful dress with long flowing hair. But they'd be surprised to learn that Sumi was in fact the **stark**▪ opposite of that image while growing up. She sported short hair and she was wildly active, running around all over the place with her friends. She looked like one of the boys. She could not stand wearing skirts or dresses.

▪ **stark** [staːrk] ⒶⓋ complete or extreme

"Sookyong, doesn't your mom buy you skirts? Why do you wear pants like a boy?"

"Why not? Can't girls wear pants? Besides, skirts are uncomfortable. I can't run or jump around in them."

"But you'll look so pretty in skirts."

"Then you go on and wear as many skirts as you want."

One day, a male classmate made fun of Sumi.

"Did you guys know? Sookyong is a boy! She's a man!"

"What? What did you say?"

"Short hair. Never wears skirts. Always playing physical games with boys. What more **proof**▪ do

▪ **proof** [pruːf] ⓝ,ⓐ any factual evidence that helps to establish the truth of something

you need?"

"You take that back."

"Make me!"

Sumi wanted to get back at that mean classmate for making fun of her. So she thought long and hard about what to do. She could just punch him, but that would be too easy. She wanted to **humiliate**▪ him. And then, she had a **brilliant**▪ idea.

Everyone was gathered outside their classrooms for the school assembly. The **headmaster**▪'s speech dragged on and everyone was very bored and tired. It was during that moment, when everyone was hungry for something exciting, Sumi snuck up to the boy who made fun of her earlier and pulled

▪ **humiliate** [hju:mílièit] Ⓥ cause to feel shame; hurt the pride of

▪ **brilliant** [bríljənt] ⓐ of surpassing excellence

▪ **headmaster** [hèdmǽstər] Ⓝ presiding officer of a school

down his pants for all to see. He **blushed**▪ and didn't know what to do, while everyone exploded with laughter. It was **pandemonium**▪ in Sumi's school yard that day.

"Sookyong! Why you little!"

"That's for calling me a boy!"

"Look! He dropped his pants!"

"Sookyong rocks! I can't believe she did that!"

"Better pull up your pants! I can see your underwear!"

Sumi paid back in ten folds, the humiliation she received from that boy. She would stand and stare down at him, and he was at her mercy. He struggled to pull his pants up, while everyone is laughing.

▪ **blush** [blʌʃ] ⓝ.ⓥ turn red, as if in embarrassment or shame
▪ **pandemonium** [pændəmóuniəm] ⓝ a state of extreme confusion and disorder

"Jo Sookyong! Why you little **rascal**■!
How could you do something like that while the
headmaster is talking! Come to the headmaster's
office now!"

The teachers had no kind words for Sumi for
her grand prank.

She had to pay the price for her behavior. The
teachers punished her by ordering her to stand with
her hands up for several hours. Although her arms
ached, the satisfaction she got from her successful
vengeance■ made her happy.

Even though she was very outgoing and loved
having fun with friends, Sumi never missed piano
practice. Knowing her daughter's musical talent

■ **rascal** [ræskl] ⓝ one who is playfully mischievous

■ **vengeance** [véndʒəns] ⓝ the act of taking revenge

well, Sumi's mother made sure Sumi received continuous piano lessons. She knew that talent is nothing without determination and hard work. When Sumi's mother had to leave home for a while, she made Sumi stay home to keep practicing the piano. Sometime she locked the door while she goes out, to make her practice piano more. Rain or shine, Sumi practiced regularly. One day, Sumi thought to herself.

'I wish I could go out and play all day like most of my friends do. Playing the piano is fun, but long hours of practice is tiring.'

She could hear her friends having fun and making a lot of noise outside her home. The

temptation▪ was too strong. Sumi began to lose focus. She would keep making mistakes. With more **silly**▪ mistakes made, Sumi became frustrated.

'Nothing's going right today. It's so annoying!'

Upset, Sumi sat in front of the piano silently. Amidst the silence, she realized something was wrong. It was too quiet at home. She snuck up to the door and slowly opened it. It wasn't locked! She looked around and discovered that her mom wasn't home. She called up her younger brothers.

"Youngjoon, Youngkoo, where's mommy?"

"She said she had to go out for a while."

"So she's not home?"

"No."

▪ **temptation** [temptéiʃən] ⓝ the desire to have or do something that you know you should avoid

▪ **silly** [síli] ⓝ,ⓐ ludicrous, foolish

Sumi let out a scream of delight! With her mom out, she was free to get out and play. She thought about it long and hard. The temptation was too strong. She called up her brothers again.

"Guys, listen up."

"What is it?"

"You know how long and hard I practice everyday, right?"

"We do."

"But sometimes, I need some **timeouts**▪. It's very tiring to practice all the time. I can't take it anymore. I'm leaving for good. Don't look for me, and if mom asks, tell her I've left and gone far and away. Okay?"

▪ **timeout** [taimaut] ⓝ a pause from doing something

The boys were taken by surprise and they began crying.

"No! Don't leave us! We'll be good."

"Guys, don't cry."

Even though her brothers cried a river and **begged**▪ her not to leave, Sumi was determined to **escape**▪. But it was late in the evening, and none of her friends were outside. Sumi walked all over the neighborhood, but none of her friends could be found. Gradually, she grew tired and hungry. As day turned to night, Sumi had little choice but to return home. Her mom spotted her trying to sneak back into the house. Sumi **braced**▪ herself to be **scolded**▪, but instead her mother welcomed

▪ **beg** [beg] ⓥ call upon in supplication

▪ **escape** [iskéip] ⓝ,ⓥ run away from confinement

▪ **brace** [breis] ⓝ,ⓥ prepare oneself for something unpleasant or difficult

▪ **scold** [skould] ⓝ,ⓥ censure severely or angrily

her with a big hug.

"Mommy?"

"Where were you? I was so worried."

"Mom..."

"It must have been difficult to practice all day. You must have missed playing with your friends. I know it is very difficult to be stuck practicing all day. I know it's hard. But Sookyong, you are so talented at singing and playing the piano. If you spend too much time outside and less on practicing, you cannot become a great musician. To be the best is not easy. But if you are going to be a musician, isn't it better to strive to be the best?"

Sumi's mother comforted her and gave her

strength to carry on. She suddenly felt ashamed of what she did that day. She was deeply touched by her mother's kind words and felt extremely bad about what she did. Upon understanding her mother's reasons for pushing her to work harder, she burst into tears. From then on, she made up her mind to be the best musician in the world.

'Mommy, I'm going to practice harder than ever!'

4. Great Ambition

Sumi was all grown up and now she was a middle schooler. To **nurture**▪ her musical talent further, she entered Sunhwa Arts School. It was a **renowned**▪ art middle school and was not too far away from her home. But before she started school, she had to decide her major. Students were only allowed to choose one.

'Piano or singing? I've practiced the piano everyday since I was little, so I'm confident of being

▪ **nurture** [nə́ːrtʃər] ⓝ,ⓥ help develop, help grow

▪ **renowned** [rináund] ⓐ widely known and esteemed

the best. But I love to sing.'

She was not alone. Her parents were also torn.

'Which one would Sookyong be able to study and be happy and be successful? Piano is her **forte**▪. But it would be a shame not to see her blossom as a singer. She has such a beautiful voice. But singing is a **risky**▪ career. She is still growing, and what if her voice changes? What should we do?'

Because Sumi was so talented in both fields, it was difficult for Sumi and her parents to make a decision. In the end, they turned to Yoo Byeongmoo, a teacher in Sumi's middle school. He welcomed them eagerly.

"Hello, I'm Sookyong."

▪ **forte** [fɔːrt] ⓝ,ⓐ an asset of special worth or utility
▪ **risky** [rìski] ⓐ involving risk or danger

"So you are. The one torn between singing and piano. Let me hear you play the piano and then sing, so I can better assist you with your decision."

"Okay. Let me play the piano first."

Sumi played the piano and it was brilliant. The teacher had nothing but praise for her.

"That's amazing. I can tell you've practiced long and hard. Now, let's hear you sing."

The teacher played the piano for Sumi to sing. Sumi sang <Leaf Boat> and he was blown away.

"The choice is clear. Sookyong should sing."

"Really?"

"She has an amazing voice. I dare say it's the most beautiful singing voice I've ever heard. She is very talented with the piano too, but it's rare to find someone who can sing like her. She will become a great singer."

"But what if her voice changes?"

"Even through that period of change, as long as she takes care of her voice, there should be no problem. We can't afford to lose an amazing voice like this!"

During **puberty**■, most teenagers experience changes in their voice. For singers, this could be a very dangerous time as their vocal talent could be **affected**■. Yoo Byeongmoo, who became Sumi's first singing **mentor**■, promised her parents that he will help take excellent care of her voice, and

■ **puberty** [pjúːbərti] ⓝ the time of life when sex glands become functional

■ **affect** [əfékt] ⓝ,ⓥ have an effect upon

■ **mentor** [méntɔːr] ⓝ,ⓥ a wise and trusted guide and advisor

strongly recommended that she pursue a career in singing. And he went above and beyond to deliver on his promise. Sumi was able to blossom into the singer she is today, thanks to good guidance from great mentors like Yoo Byeongmoo during her teenage years. Another great mentor in Sumi's life is professor Lee Gyeongsook of Seoul National University. Having learned so much under the **tutelage**[■] of Mr. Yoo in middle school, Sumi improved by leaps and bounds by the time she entered high school. Mr. Yoo felt that Sumi needed a new teacher to help push her to new heights. He called up Sumi to talk to her.

"Sookyong, in my opinion you are ready to

■ **tutelage** [tjúːtəlidʒ] ⓝ teaching pupils individually

learn more than what I can teach you. There is a professor from Seoul National University named Lee Gyeongsook. She can teach you to improve even further. I'll let her know you are coming."

Professor Lee was one of the best sopranos in Korea during those days. There were countless students eager to learn from her, waiting in line. Sumi now had a chance to learn from such a great teacher. But professor Lee was also **notorious**[*] for being very strict and harsh. Naturally Sumi was extremely nervous to meet her. Her heart began to beat faster and she began **sweating**[*] in fear and anxiety.

"I've heard about you Sookyong. Try and relax.

[*] **notorious** [noutɔ́:riəs] ⓐ known widely and usually unfavorably

[*] **sweat** [swet] ⓝ,ⓥ excrete perspiration through the pores in the skin

Okay, let's hear it."

"Okay."

Sumi calmed her nerves and performed flawlessly. Professor Lee didn't say a word after Sumi finished singing. She simply walked up to Sumi and hugged her tightly.

"Sookyong. You have **tremendous** talent. You have what it takes to become the best not just in Korea but the world."

"Thank you."

Sumi was speechless after receiving such great compliments from Korea's best soprano. Sumi could feel that the teacher had great love and faith in her. Sumi was grateful to the professor. From then on,

■ **tremendous** [triméndəs] ⓐ extraordinarily good or great

Sumi took weekly lessons from professor Lee. The most important lesson she learned was on how to find her true voice.

"The search for one's own true voice is a long and difficult process. It's like looking for the perfect seashell of your choice in a long stretch of the beach. There are so many of them in so many different shapes and sizes, so it's not easy to find the one that's perfect for you. The same applies to voices. You can only find the best and the most ideal voice for you only after countless practice, trial and error."

Thanks to professor Lee's teachings, Sumi was able to improve immensely and use her voice with greater control. Sumi was searching hard in the **vast**▪ ocean for the right seashell. Just as the professor said in the early parts of her lessons, the search was long and difficult. But Sumi enjoyed every part of the process, as it gave her great joy.

▪ **vast** [væst] ⓐ unusually great in size or amount or degree or especially extent or scope

5. Days of Being Wild and Lost

After completing high school, Sumi entered Seoul National University to major in classical vocal music. The school offered the best music program in Korea, and Sumi was the most impressive **candidate** that year. Among the students that auditioned for the school, she received the highest score in the school's history up to that point. She became an instant celebrity. Her **peers** were

---

■ **candidate** [kǽndidèit] ⓝ someone who is considered for something for an office or honor

■ **peer** [piər] ⓝ,ⓥ a person who is of equal standing with another in a group

either **awed**▪ or green with envy. The professors' expectations of her grew and grew. And that's how her college year began. College life was something very new and strange to Sumi. Compared to the **hectic**▪ schedule she was accustomed to, campus life was so laid back. It was a whole new world. She felt lost as it seemed like a much bigger **arena**▪ than the one she was accustomed to. All the freedom to do anything she desires. It was unfamiliar territory for Sumi, who knew nothing but music and practice.

"Sookyong! Join us for a group blind date!"

"Let's skip class and have some fun outside!"

"Let's go clubbing tonight! Join us!"

Temptation was lurking everywhere. Sumi

▪ **awe** [ɔː] ⓝ.ⓥ a feeling of profound respect for someone or something

▪ **hectic** [héktik] ⓐ marked by intense agitation or emotion

▪ **arena** [ərí:nə] ⓝ a particular environment or walk of life

could not say no to a lot of them. She always had a tendency to focus on one thing only. Her ability to shut out everything else and focus on one particular activity is helpful in her musical training. So when she opened her eyes to other activities, she became very focused on those activities as well. Hanging out with friends and having fun became her priority. She **neglected**■ music, practice and school work and focused on having fun. Her parents and teachers were concerned. But they had faith in her. They believed that she will find her way back, so they didn't **intervene**■. But Sumi was too immature to note that they let her be because they trusted her.

■ **neglect** [niglékt] ⓝ,ⓥ give little or no attention to

■ **intervene** [intərvíːn] ⓥ get involved, so as to alter or hinder an action, or through force or threat of force

There was one significant event that stands out during Sumi's college years. Her first crush. He was a business major in the same university. He was tall and handsome, and Sumi could not stop thinking about him. After pondering about what to do for days, she decided to take action. Sumi walked up to him and said.

"Hi, I'm Jo Sookyong. I major in singing. Would you like to go out with me? Call me if you want to. Okay?"

Although she seemed cool and calm on the outside, Sumi was very nervous. The boy was surprised to be asked out by a girl, so suddenly. A few days later he called and they began dating.

Sumi was a very devoted girlfriend. Because of her tendency to focus only on one thing, other than the relationship, nothing else mattered. She had no time for school or music. She would devote her time to him. Nothing else seemed to matter. She was completely head over heels in love with him.

But her days of being **distracted**" was about to come to an end. Professor Lee decided to give Sumi a wake-up call. Sumi was talented enough to sing any piece well after just going through it once. And she continued to do just that. Professor Lee **snapped**" at Sumi.

"Seriously! You better wake up!"

Sumi was shocked and **frightened**" by the

■ **distract** [distrǽkt] ⓥ disturb in mind or make uneasy or cause to be worried or alarmed

■ **snap** [snæp] ⓝ,ⓥ utter in an angry, sharp, or abrupt tone

■ **fright** [frait] ⓝ,ⓥ cause fear in

professor's burst of anger. Sumi has never seen her this angry before.

"I know you just browse through the music sheets once before you come to me. Maybe other people can't tell, but I can. You've gone too far. You are **mocking**▪ my class by doing that. Get out!"

It appears the professor knew exactly what was going on with Sumi. Initially she kept quiet and let Sumi be, as she had faith in her diligent student. But her patience finally ran out. As Sumi thought about nothing but her relationship with her boyfriend, her parents and teacher were deeply concerned.

"Sookyong, think about all you've worked for to get this far. What is wrong with you these days?

▪ **mock** [mak] ⓐ,ⓝ,ⓥ treat with contempt

I trusted you to at least focus on your music even if we gave you freedom to do whatever you want with your time. Your grades are failing! Is it because of your boyfriend?"

"Mother, I want to marry him."

"What did you say?"

"I can be happy with him. Then I won't need music in my life."

"Sookyong…"

"I've made up my mind. You can't force me out of this decision."

"Have you given this enough thought? I know he is an important part of your life now. But music has been a big part of your life too. Have you forgotten how much you loved it? You should take some time to think about what really matters to you and what can make you happy in the long run."

Sumi's parents and her teacher decided to talk to Sumi about studying abroad.

"You wanted to talk to me, professor?"

"Have a seat. You know your grades have suffered greatly, right?"

"Yes. I know."

"I've known you since high school and I'm still certain that you have an amazing musical talent. A world-class talent in fact. I love you very much and I want the best for you. I feel that this might be a good time for you to study outside of this country."

"Leave Korea?"

"Italy has some of the top music schools in the world. And if you plan to become the best singer in the world, I feel that studying in Italy is a necessity. Over there, you will regain your passion for music, and learn to be the best."

"But I don't want to leave Korea."

"It's your decision. I want you to think about it."

Sumi finally realized how badly she disappointed her parents and teacher. She felt terrible for hurting them by not living up to their expectations. Sumi realized this: she assumed that she had talent enough to take it easy. Realizing how **arrogant**, lazy and **selfish** she has been, Sumi became angry at herself.

■ **arrogant** [ǽrəgənt] ⓐ having or showing feelings of unwarranted importance out of overbearing pride

■ **selfish** [sélfiʃ] ⓐ concerned chiefly or only with yourself and your advantage to the exclusion of others

One day, on her way back from school, Sumi noticed her mother waiting for her at the bus stop. Sumi's mother who had unshakable faith in her daughter grabbed Sumi's hands and said to her.

"Sookyong, if music gave you nothing but pain, I want you to quit. I just wanted you to be happy, and I thought music brought you happiness. I knew your songs will make many people in the world happy. But perhaps I was wrong. I'm sorry if I forced you to do something that made life difficult for you."

Sumi felt awful. Not only did she disappoint her mom and herself, she turned her back on the one thing that used to make her happy: music.

She had to make up her mind. She decided to talk to her boyfriend about the matter.

"My parents and my teacher recommended studying abroad."

"I see."

"What do you think?"

"If it's necessary, you should go."

Sumi was deeply **wounded**▪ by his words. She was hoping that he would ask her to stay. Sumi thought about it.

'Why wouldn't he ask me to stay? Perhaps he feels there are more important things for us than each other. He feels that music is more important in my life than him. Perhaps he's right.'

▪ **wounded** [wú:ndid] ⓝ,ⓐ suffering from injury

It was a difficult decision, but Sumi decided it was for the best. As she thought it over, she could understand where her boyfriend was coming from. She became determined to study abroad. Sumi swore to work harder than ever to make up for lost time and so that she can return the love and support she received.

6. Flames of the Piazza Venezia at Dawn

On her flight to Italy, Sumi felt uneasy. She couldn't stop thinking about her boyfriend. The idea of starting fresh in a foreign country filled her with hopes and fears. But more than anything, she felt bad about how her family could barely afford her flight tickets. They really went above and beyond to scrap enough money to buy the tickets, just 3 days before her departure. Sumi was grateful for her parents for their love and faith, and felt terribly sorry for making them pay for her expensive ventures.

Her plane landed in Rome late at night. It was raining. Noticing only foreigners all around her, it finally sank in. She was alone in a strange land. The darkness and the **dampness**[■] didn't help make things better. To make matters worse, the person who was supposed to pick her up at the airport failed to show up. After waiting for a long time, she decided to find her way to her quarters.

'Fine. I can do it by myself. This is my new home anyway. So I might as well get a head start in familiarizing the place.'

She hailed a cab and told the driver where

■ **dampness** [dǽmpnis] ⓝ a slight wetness

she wants to go in English. But the driver did not understand English. So she used her basic knowledge of the Italian language to ask the driver to take her to any hotel near the Piazza Venezia. She checked in, left her luggage in her room and came out of the hotel. It was too late or too early for people to be out and about. So the streets were empty. Sumi just walked aimlessly. Everything was new and strange. The damp air, the scent of the surroundings and the dead silence. She already missed her mother. She missed how her mother would wait for her at the bus stop and give her a warm hug.

'I wonder what my family's doing right now.

I still can't believe I'm here all alone.'

After walking aimlessly for hours, she ended up in the Piazza Venezia. Sumi took in a deep breath and then began singing in **tunes**■ that are familiar to the locals. While doing so she gradually felt more at home. Two **torches**■ were burning bright. While staring at the flames, she made a promise to herself.

'It's a fresh start for me. I'm not going to be distracted. I will focus solely on my music. Just like this torch, I will light up the stage. I am Sookyong. I'm Sookyong from Korea. I will be the best opera singer in the world.'

First thing she did upon returning to her room was to take out her diary. Writing about her day

---

■ **tune** [tjuːn] Ⓝ,Ⓥ a melody or melodic line
■ **torch** [tɔːrʧ] Ⓝ,Ⓥ a light usually carried in the hand

became routine for her. Writing down her thoughts helped her remember them and stay on course towards her goals. She was more determined than ever.

• Never cry or grow weak, no matter what kind of hardships come my way.

• Never show signs of weakness or loneliness. Always stay proud and confident.

• Focus all my energy in studying music and languages.

• Stay clean, tidy and organized.

• Be wary of people and their words. Always say and do what I mean.

Sumi kept busy the entire day, everyday. She had to juggle mastering foreign languages and music. She even changed her name to Sumi, so her classmates can **pronounce**▪ her name with ease. Many suggested using an English name, but Sumi wanted to maintain her Korean identity. She was focused only in her studies. She even spent less time sleeping and eating, just to study a little extra. Accademia di Santa Cecilia, where Sumi studied, was full of talented students. She realized that she had to study and practice hard just to keep up with the others. Even at home she spent many hours practicing her projection. For making so much noise with her singing practice,

▪ **pronounce** [prənáuns] ⓥ speak, pronounce, or utter in a certain way

she was **evicted**▪ more than 7 times in one year.

After moving countless times, Sumi finally settled down in a place run by an old lady. Every resident called her 'Mama'. She was very strict but very caring. Her place was beautiful and she always played classical music. Most importantly, Mama loved music, so she was perfectly okay with Sumi practicing as loud as she wanted to.

"Sumi! Make your bed before you join us for breakfast!"

"Sumi! Your room's a **mess**▪! It's a pig pen!"

"Sumi! You should practice cooking! You've burned all my pots!"

Mama may **nag**▪ often but she loved Sumi

▪ **evict** [ivikt] Ⓥ expel or eject without recourse to legal process

▪ **mess** [mes] Ⓝ,Ⓥ a state of confusion and disorderliness

▪ **nag** [næg] Ⓝ,Ⓥ bother persistently with trivial complaints

like her own grand-daughter. Since Sumi never lived with her grandparents, so Mama became the grandmother she never had. But life in Italy was a little more demanding than Korean life, as Sumi had to do everything by herself. She had to manage her time wisely to get everything done, including studying the language, cooking, doing the laundry and practicing. Sumi's day was always full of all kinds of work to be done.

Sumi studied under soprano Lucia Valentini of Rome Civil Opera and Giannella Borelli of Accademia di Santa Cecilia. It got really hot in Italy and taking public transportation to attend lessons was a very draining task. But Sumi hung in there.

As time went on, Sumi adapted well to her new life. Making her bed and tidying up her room well became routine for her. Mama had nothing but praise for Sumi.

"Sumi, you're all grown up now!"

Because of her hectic daily schedule, **skipping**▪meals or sleeping less became common practice.

One day, she blacked out while walking on the streets. She opened her eyes in the hospital later that day. The doctor told her.

"You've got **anemia**▪ and **gastritis**▪. It's amazing how you could actually do all the things you do everyday in such a condition. From now on,

▪ **skip** [skip] ⓝ,ⓥ bypass

▪ **anemia** [əníːmiə] ⓝ a deficiency of red blood cells

▪ **gastritis** [gæstráitis] ⓝ inflammation of the lining of the stomach

make sure you get plenty of iron in your diet. You need to eat more meat."

"But other than that I'm okay right? I'll still be able to sing?"

Sumi, suddenly gripped with fear, began to cry. The doctor calmed her down.

"Don't worry, it's okay. You're just very physically drained and weak right now. You need to take better care of yourself and eat well. Never skip meals. If you want to sing well, you must stay healthy."

Sumi was **homesick**[■]. She missed the family and friends back home. She missed Korea, and Korean food. She was extremely lonely, having

■ **homesick** [hóumsik] ⓐ longing to return home

no one to talk to after a long, hard day. Her 20th birthday was approaching, and **aggravated**▪ her loneliness. The night before her birthday, Sumi cried a river. The next day, Sumi got out of bed, packed her bag and headed out to school, as if nothing happened the night before. Birthday or no birthday, practice is still on.

"Sumi, is today your birthday?"

A Korean student studying in the same school approached Sumi. She was taken by surprise.

"How did you...?"

"You're so bright and outgoing all the time, but your eyes are swollen and you look so **glum**▪. I can tell in an instant. I know how that feels like.

▪ **aggravate** [ǽgrəvèit] ⓥ make worse

▪ **glum** [glʌm] ⓐ moody and melancholic

I remember my first birthday away from home in this country."

"Oh..."

"Let's go to my place after class. I'll cook seaweed soup for you. No Korean birthday is complete without it!"

Sumi was extremely grateful for her kind gesture. While having soup, Sumi cried again. This time, they weren't tears of loneliness or sorrow, they were tears of joy and gratefulness.

7. A Momentary Despair, a Prelude to the Big Break

One day, one of her teachers, Valentini came to talk to Sumi about participating in international singing competitions.

"Sumi, you should take part in some vocal competition."

"Me?"

"Yes. You have what it takes to compete. But to prepare for international competitions, you need to sing French arias or German lied. So let's take part in domestic competitions in Italy first."

"Okay, I'll work hard and prepare well."

Sumi was focused on finding out ways to become the best performer she can be. She practiced day and night, and her efforts paid off. She was able to showcase her talent in the school's recital.

After the recital, a special guest approached her.

"Hi, I'm John Scannell, a composer. You were amazing out there. There is someone I'd like you to meet."

"Thank you. I'm **flattered**▪ and delighted to hear that. Who do you want me to meet?"

John introduced Sumi to Austrian soprano

▪ **flatter** [flǽtər] ⓥ praise somewhat dishonestly

Margaret Baker. She expressed willingness to help Sumi prepare for international competitions. This was a great proposition for Sumi. Margaret, who is skilled at performing in French and German taught Sumi to sing French arias and German lieds.

Sumi was clearly talented, as she was able to master Italian opera, French aria and German lied. She was ready for the big competitions. Her first choice was one held in Finland in 1984. There she stood out from the rest and various media praised this phenomenal performer. Some of the headlines read: "Sumi is sure to win!", "The youngest performer from Korea!"

Most experts also predicted that Sumi will win

the competition easily. Sumi was convinced that this was her time to shine. But to everyone's surprise, a Finnish singer took home the trophy. Sumi was crushed.

'I don't believe it. It was as if I was the sure winner.'

It could be that the Finnish singer had the home advantage and therefore earned extra points. But Sumi was so devastated. The incident was enough to make her lose her passion for singing. Her mother wrote a letter to her to **console**■ her.

"Sookyong, I never asked you to sing to win competitions. Music is something beautiful. A good song is able to **soothe**■ the soul. If a singer is full of

■ **console** [kənsóul] ⓝ,ⓥ give moral or emotional strength to
■ **soothe** [suːð] ⓥ cause to feel better

anger and **remorse**▪, her song will never shine. I just want you to be able to sing with joy and love. That's all I want."

The letter was just what Sumi needed to gain strength to carry on. Sumi decided to fall in love with music all over again, and then prepare for other international singing competitions. She wanted to get better and gain greater recognition for her singing capabilities. First, she won the international concours: Napoli Zonta. And that signaled the beginning of a long winning streak for Sumi. She was crowned in many more international competitions: Sicily Enna, Vercelli Viotti, Vinas, Barcelona; Pretoria, South Africa;

▪ **remorse** [rimɔ́ːrs] ⓝ a feeling of deep regret

and Verona, Italy. It only took two and a half years for her to get her diploma from Santa Cecilia Music Conservatory. This **sensational**[■] performer from Asia was gaining greater recognition everyday.

In 1986, Sumi made her international debut as 'Gilda' in Verdi's opera <Rigoletto> at Trieste Opera. The major cast of the opera <Rigoletto> are Rigoletto, a jester in the court of the Duke of Mantua and the daughter of Rigoletto, Gilda. The story is set in 16th century Northern Italy. The Duke is a playboy who **vows**[■] to have his way with Gilda. Rigoletto plots to kill the Duke as he doesn't want to lose his daughter to him. But Gilda falls in love with the Duke, and tragically Rigoletto ends

■ **sensational** [senséiʃənl] ⓐ causing intense interest, curiosity, or emotion

■ **vow** [vau] ⓝ,ⓥ make a vow; promise

up killing his daughter. Rigoletto falls into despair, driven by **guilt**▪.

Sumi loved this piece ever since she was little. And this was the role of a lifetime for her as an opera singer. Just thinking about going on stage to play a part in this piece made her heart pound harder than ever. It was her turn to shine. The audience fell in love with her character, brought to life by her extraordinary voice. They could feel what the character felt and by the time the opera reached its climax of Gilda's tragic death in her father's arms, Sumi received a standing **ovation**▪. Her stage debut was a roaring success.

After her debut, Sumi returned to Korea to

▪ **guilt** [gilt] ⓝ the state of having committed an offense
▪ **ovation** [ouvéiʃən] ⓝ enthusiastic recognition especially one accompanied by loud applause

spend the year's end with her family for the first time. It's been 3 years since she came to Italy to study. She instantly burst into tears when she saw her parents at the airport. The whole family hurdled and cried during that moment of reunion. They spent quite some time, crying tears of joy and helping to wipe each other's cheeks. Sumi was so happy to have the time to visit her hometown after her long journey to become an opera prima donna. It was a well deserved reward after 3 long years of nothing but hard work and dedication in a foreign land.

But suddenly Sumi caught a cold. Perhaps the sudden change in the climate after coming to

Korea was partly to be blamed. Catching a cold or flu could be fatal to an opera singer. If the vocal cord get **swollen**▪, one will not be able to sing. The idea of not being able to sing struck fear into Sumi's heart. She was due to perform in Rome in a short while. But even if her mom tended to her with love and care, she didn't get better.

"What should we do? Will it be okay to return to Rome like this?"

"It's okay mom. There's no turning back. I have to perform. I'll visit a hospital as soon as I get to Rome. Don't worry."

When she visited a hospital in Rome after her return to Rome, the doctor told her.

▪ **swell** [swel] ⓐ,ⓝ,ⓥ increase in size, magnitude, number, or intensity

"You've caught a cold and you have bronchitis. Your throat is swollen. This must hurt a lot."

"You mean I can't sing?"

"Sing? You shouldn't even be talking! If you want to get better, you'd better take my advice and have a good rest."

Sumi's mind was blank. Unable to do the only thing she has devoted her whole life to. There was no harsher punishment for Sumi than this. Just when she thought she had it made and earned a chance to relax, this happens. She feared for the worst. And the worst came to be. Sumi had to pass on the promised performance that spring.

She was supposed to perform in a recital in

the Republic of South Africa. And since she failed to perform once, she didn't want to let her fans down again. But perhaps she pushed herself too hard. She reached a point where she couldn't even speak. She also suffered from a fever of 40 degrees celsius. In the end she had to cancel again. Pain seemed to greet her in all corners. Ultimately, she had to cancel all her performances scheduled up to July that year. For half a year, she was unable to sing.

Through this painful experience, Sumi learned the importance of taking very good care of herself. As an opera singer good self-maintenance is just as important a duty as training and performing.

She would always keep her instrument warm with mufflers, drink warm water or tea regularly, wear thick socks to keep her body warm, avoid food with too much spice, salt or other condiments, and get plenty of sleep. Making sure she doesn't change her daily routine was very important. This was to make sure her bio-rhythm won't be disrupted, wherever she maybe. It wasn't easy, but to make sure she can do what she loves and never disappoint her fans around the world, she had to make sure she is professional on and off the stage.

8. Oh! Maestro!

Sumi had a most promising start to a brilliant career. She became the soprano that gained **incredible**▪ international **recognition**▪ in a hurry. There were calls from everywhere inviting her to perform and even reprising the role of Gilda in <Rigoletto>. It all felt like a dream to Sumi. Sumi believed she was being richly rewarded for the tough times she endured while studying and

▪ **incredible** [inkrédəbl] ⓐ beyond belief or understanding
▪ **recognition** [rèkəgníʃən] ⓝ the state or quality of being recognized or acknowledged

struggling to make it in the opera world. She was busier than ever practicing and performing. And she loved every moment of it. Sumi trained hard, performed with great energy and conditioned herself well. She was becoming a professional's professional.

1988 was an important year for Sumi. Because that's when she first met legendary conductor, Herbert von Karajan. This Austrian orchestra and opera conductor is regarded as one of the most **influential**▪ figures in 20th century classical music. Karajan heard great things about the impressive **petite**▪ Asian soprano. And he called her up to find out for himself. Sumi could not believe it.

▪ **influential** [ìnfluénʃəl] ⓐ having or exercising influence or power
▪ **petite** [pətíːt] ⓝ,ⓐ very small

She prepared hard and flew all the way to Salzburg, Austria for an audition. Karajan was physically weak, and he needed an assistant to help him walk. Though small in stature, his presence alone was enough to make Sumi very nervous. Sumi performed a part from <Rigoletto>. She has sung it a thousand times before, but with the great Karajan watching, Sumi was shaking. Karajan called Sumi up and talked to her.

"Unbelievable. That was amazing. Where did you learn to sing?"

"I'm Korean and I first learned how to sing in Korea."

"Impossible! That tiny country produced a

beautiful soprano such as you! Korea must be a land full of great teachers. Your voice is a gift from heaven. Voice like yours comes only once in maybe a century. Take good care of your voice and keep on singing beautiful songs!"

Sumi jumped with joy upon hearing such great praise from Karajan. It came as quite a surprise since he is known to be a stern and harsh critic. Karajan loved Sumi and cared for her as if she is the daughter he never had. He even promised to perform with her.

"I want you to play the role of Oscar in Verdi's opera, <Un Ballo in Maschera(A Masked Ball)> during the Salzburg Festival."

"That would be a great honor for me."

The operatic piece is based on the **assassination**[■] of King Gustav III of Sweden. Riccardo, Earl of Warwick and governor of Boston falls in love with Amelia, wife of Renato, who is Riccardo's secretary, best friend and confidant. One day, a fortune teller warns Riccardo that the first person he shake hands with on that day will take his life. Renato shakes Riccardo's hand first on that day. Renato finds out that Riccardo is in love with his wife, and ends up killing Riccardo out of anger.

Sumi's character Oscar, Riccardo's page is a charming, lovely character that sings many cheerful songs.

■ **assassination** [əsæsənéiʃən] ⓝ murder of a public figure by surprise attack

Sumi learned a great deal under Karajan's guidance. Although Karajan was stern and strict with everyone, he was extremely gentle and kind to Sumi. He taught Sumi meticulously, down to the smallest hand gesture. Sumi did all she can to learn everything Karajan taught her.

It was July, just days before <A Masked Ball> opened. There was no practice schedule for that day, so she stayed home and watched TV. Every channel was showing a special program dedicated to Karajan. Sumi sensed something was wrong. After the special features followed breaking news, informing viewers of Karajan's death. Sumi watched in disbelief. Some of her cast and crew members came by soon after. They cried together for hours. Sumi noticed Karajan's health was rapidly declining before this happened, so she felt partly responsible for his death. She wished she spent less time taking lessons from him and more time checking up on his health.

"I don't think I can play the part of Oscar in <A Masked Ball>. Without Maestro Karajan, this opera is meaningless to me."

Sumi went up to conductor Georg Solti, who substituted Karajan and told him she no longer wanted to be a part of the performance. But Solti would not allow that to happen. He kindly talked to Sumi.

"Sumi, I feel your pain. We all feel the same way. But without you, this show would be even more meaningless. Karajan loved you dearly. He wouldn't want anyone else playing Oscar. Pull yourself together and let's do it. Let's do it for Karajan."

Sumi was **convinced** ▪.

'Karajan would want me to play Oscar. I'll thank him for all he's done for me by putting up my very best performance.'

Sumi practiced harder than ever. She would think of Karajan and keep on pushing herself. Even on opening night, she was still very emotional, as memories of Karajan **lingered** ▪.

▪ **convince** [kənvíns] ⓥ make agree, understand, or realize the truth or validity of something

▪ **linger** [líŋɡər] ⓥ remain present although waning or gradually dying

But she recalled Karajan's advice, to focus only on the music and nothing else on stage. <A Masked Ball> was a huge success. Sumi was not alone. Everyone performed hard in memory of the late Karajan. Sumi gained even greater recognition and respect for her performance.

9. A True Artist

Jo Sumi became the first Asian prima donna to perform in 5 major opera theaters in the world. These include La Scala in Milano, Italy, Royal Opera House in London, England, Bastille Opera in Paris, France, New York's Metropolitan Opera House and Staatsoper in Wien, Austria. It is considered a tremendous honor for an opera singer to have performed in just one of these prestigious venues. And that proves how respected Jo Sumi is in the industry.

In 1993 at the sixth La Siola d'Oro, honoring the greatest in opera, Sumi was named the best soprano of the year. Also, that same year, she won a Grammy award for a recording of R. Strauss's <Die Frau ohne Schatten(Woman without a Shadow)> which she collaborated with conductor Solti. The Grammy is considered to be the highest musical honor in America. It was clear after winning these awards, that Sumi has blossomed into one of the best sopranos in the world. No matter how successful she became, Sumi took great pride in her Korean **heritage** . Unfortunately during

---

■ **heritage** [héritidʒ] ⓝ any attribute or immaterial possession that is inherited from ancestors

those days, most Europeans knew little about Korea. Every time she performed, she informed her audience that she is Korean and then gave a detailed introduction of Korea. She always tried to wear traditional Korean costume, 'Hanbok' to better promote her home country. And then one day, after she performed a concert in Korea, renowned fashion designer, Andre Kim came to meet her after watching the concert.

"Sumi, thank you for that marvelous performance. It was beautiful and fantastic. I want to express my gratitude for this wonderful experience with my dresses. I would like to present you with dresses to wear for all your future performances."

"That would be wonderful. I would be honored to wear your dresses."

The late Andre Kim is a legendary figure in Korea's fashion scene. He was so moved by Sumi's performance, that he decided to show his appreciation in the best way he can. It was a very generous proposal and a timely one in fact, as Sumi did find it difficult to choose and purchase expensive dresses for each concert. As promised, Andre Kim provides Sumi with his dresses. Each dress was designed with specific performance in mind. For over 20 years, Sumi wore nothing but Andre Kim's dresses. They were **vivid** ▪, beautiful

▪ **vivid** [vívid] ⓐ evoking lifelike images within the mind and always included uniquely Korean elements. They brought out the best in Sumi and the performances. Foreign media not only praised Sumi's performance, but her sense of style.

Even though Sumi seemed to be at the peak of her career, she never stopped taking on new challenges and pushing herself to get better. There is an operatic piece titled <Ariadne auf Naxos(Ariadne on Naxos)> composed by Richard Strauss in 1912. But the key was too high for any sopranos to reach. No one could sing it. In the end, the key was lowered. And after 1916, the original was forgotten as only the revised version was used. But Sumi wanted to try the original pitch.

"Sumi, you have nothing to prove. Everyone knows how talented you are already. Don't do it. No one has been able to do it."

"It's not because I want to prove I'm better than anyone. It's just a challenge I need to take on."

But it seemed like an impossible challenge. Sumi thought about giving up, but she felt she has come too far. And in 1994, she succeeded. She became the first soprano in the world to perform that impossible piece. Sumi pondered about new ways to bring joy to people through music.

She believed that music should **transcend**▪ boundaries instead of being confined to the shells of classics or fine arts. She believed music, regardless

▪ **transcend** [trænsénd] ⓥ be superior or better than some standard

of genre is something beautiful. She recalled the struggles to get better during a young age. She still found room for improvement even after becoming one of the best opera singers in the world.

Sumi wanted to make opera more approachable to people who weren't accustomed to it. And so she began planning concerts and recording new albums with this purpose in mind. She even expanded her **repertoire**▪ to musicals, K-pop, folk songs and theme songs for TV dramas. Something no opera singer in the past has done before. In 2002 and 2006, Sumi sang the cheer songs for the World Cup. People loved her powerful voice and inspirational cheer songs. Thanks to her efforts, more people

---

▪ **repertoire** [répərtwὰːr] ⓝ the entire range of skills or aptitudes or devices used in a particular field or occupation

could appreciate classical music and opera with ease.

In 2007, Sumi was designated UNESCO Artist for Peace in recognition of her commitment to the promotion of music, culture and peace. In 2010 Sumi was named Goodwill Ambassador for the Korean Red Cross and held charity Christmas concerts. All proceeds were donated to the Red Cross. Sumi stuck with her goal of spreading love and joy to more people through her music. And still today, she makes time to get involved in such charitable efforts, on and off stage.

In 2008, Sumi became the first non-Italian singer to win the International Puccini Award. This **prestigious** award goes only to those who

---

■ **prestigious** [prestídʒəs] ⓐ having an illustrious reputation; respected

contributed greatly to promoting Italian operas to the world. There could not be a greater honor for an opera singer. And that happened to be the 150th anniversary of Puccini and the year of promoting greater cultural ties between Korea and Italy. What's remarkable is the fact that Sumi became the first foreigner to win this award.

10. Farewell Father

It was 2006. To mark the 20th anniversary of her debut, Sumi was about to perform at the Chatelet Theater Paris, France. Right before she went on stage, she received a call.

"This is Sumi."

"Sister, it's me, Youngjoon."

The call was from her brother in Korea. Sumi was excited to hear his voice.

"Hey, how are you? How is mom and dad? Listen, I have to get on stage soon."

"Dad... passed away."

"What?"

She felt like her world was crumbling down. Sumi felt **nauseated**▪ and almost collapsed, but she gathered herself. She desperately prayed for this to be a prank call from his brother. She did not want this to be true. But her brother's reply was the same.

"We just thought you should know. You just focus on your performance and come back to us when you're done. We'll take care of the funeral."

"No. I'm going there right now. Wait for me."

▪ **nauseated** [nɔ́ːzièited] ⓐ feeling nausea; feeling about to vomit

Sumi was in no condition to perform. Her mind was blank. Her father, worked hard just to support Sumi's dreams. He was always smiling and had nothing but praise for Sumi. He sacrificed everything to make sure Sumi could study in Italy and get a good start to her amazing career. How she wished she spent more time with him. Sumi was so caught up with her hectic schedule that she barely got to spend enough time with her family with her dad. But now, he has left her. Sumi could not regain her composure.

"Sookyong, it's me, your mom."

"Don't disappoint your fans who made time and travelled far to watch your performance. I'm sure your dad would have wanted you to stick to your responsibility as a performer. We'll take care of things here. You just get out there and focus on your responsibility."

Sumi decided to listen to her mother's stern request, and hung up the phone. Just like how she dedicated <A Masked Ball> to Maestro Karajan when he passed away, she decided to dedicate this performance to her father. It was extremely difficult for her to perform much less stand in her state of emotion. Her eyes welled up with tears, and it was hard for her not to break down during the performance. But she did it. The audience responded with **thunderous**▪ applause and calls

▪ **thunderous** [θʌndərəs] ⓐ loud enough to cause hearing loss

for an encore. Sumi, with tears flowing down her cheek addressed them.

"Even as I speak, right now, in my home country, Korea, my father's funeral is being held. Upon hearing the news of my father's passing before the show, I did not think I could even stand on this stage today. But my father would not have wanted me to break my promise to you as a performer.
So I went on with the show. And now, I would like to take a moment to remember and honor him.
I dedicate today's performance and this song to my father, who will be listening in heaven."

For her father Sumi sang Franz Schubert's

<Ave Maria>.

"Ave Maria, Maiden mild. Oh, listen to a maiden's prayer. For thou canst hear amid the wild. 'Tis thou, 'tis thou canst save amid, despair."

As her song ended, the crowd, all in tears, got on their feet and gave an emotional standing ovation to Sumi. For over 10 minutes they spared no effort in sending their gratitude, love and warmth to the heartbroken artist.

11. For Love and Peace

Jo Sumi believes that her most important duty is to make people happy through her songs. The path towards reaching such a level in the music industry is long and hard. Sumi made a promise to herself, and she did everything to keep that promise. And even today, she continues walking that same path to give people joy. As an opera singer, she has achieved almost everything there is to achieve. But she still seeks out new challenges. She doesn't limit her range to just classical music. She will use her talent in any way possible to provide music lovers with a chance to have a great time. In her diary she wrote.

'I see myself as a bird, flying all around the globe, singing songs of love and peace. During my journey I would get hurt, I will face strong winds and would have to shield myself behind large trees. Each time I am trying to fly higher and further. And everytime I'm in despair, I think about my mother and the people I love. The temptation to return to the comfort of my nest is always there. But for 30 years, I kept on flapping my wings and kept on going. And now I know where I must go and how to get there. I have no fear now. I know there will be hard times again. But I am richly rewarded when I fly across the world, taking in the beauty and wonders of all parts of our world, and spreading joy and happiness to the people I meet.'

영어로 읽는 세계 속 한국인 ❻

SUMI JO 조수미

초판 1쇄 인쇄 2013년 4월 15일
초판 1쇄 발행 2013년 4월 20일

지은이	Daniel Choy(최진완), Yun Hyeji(윤혜지)
펴낸이	이준경
편집	박윤선
디자인	김인엽
마케팅	오정옥
펴낸곳	(주)영진미디어
출판등록	2011년 1월 7일 제141-81-22416

주소	경기도 파주시 문발동 파주출판도시 504-3 (주)영진미디어
전화	031-955-4955
팩스	031-955-4959
이메일	book@yjmedia.net
홈페이지	www.yjbooks.com
종이	(주)월드페이퍼
인쇄	(주)현문자현
녹음	(주)미디어뱅크포유
음악감독	김형석

값 12,000원
ISBN 978-89-98656-03-4

* 본 시리즈의 영문 이름 표기법은 정부에서 권장하는 한글 고유 어순 표기법에 따르고 있으나
〈조수미〉편의 경우 소속사의 요청에 따라 표제에 이름, 성 순으로 영문 표기하였습니다.